SPIRITUAL RECIPE

A Simple Guide for Your Spiritual Awakening

ROBIN WHITT

ROBIN WHITT

Printed in the United States of America
First Printing 2020
First Edition 2020

ISBN 978-1-7359619-0-3

10 9 8 7 6 5 4 3 2 1

The information provided within this book is for general informational and educational purposes only. Although the author and publisher have made every effort to ensure that the information in this book was correct at press time, the author and publisher do not assume and hereby disclaim any liability to any party for any loss, damage, or disruption caused by errors and omissions, whether such errors or omissions result from negligence, accident, or any other cause. This book is not intended as a substitute for the medical advice of physicians.

www.spriritualrecipe.com

I joyfully dedicate this book to my amazing family. Jimmy, Jesse, Jordan, Valerie, and Elizabeth, I write these words for you in hopes that they will bring overwhelming love and light into your lives.

TABLE OF CONTENTS

FOREWORD

This is an inspiring guide based on real experiences and profound science and spirituality. Truths that will help you with some familiar and *"aha"* moments. This is definitely a seed of motivation on anyone's journey. No matter your spiritual beliefs!

-Rev. Rosebud Cherokee Rose

INTRODUCTION

You have to grow from the inside out. None can teach you; none can make you spiritual. There is no other teacher but your own soul." - Swami Vivekananda

Let me be clear up front: I do not have a Ph.D. and do not claim to be any sort of expert. What I do have is experience. I have been through my own spiritual awakening. I know that I have gained knowledge and wisdom that I can share to help others. My thoughts and beliefs aren't new. Albert Einstein, Ralph Waldo Emerson, Dr. Wayne Dyer, Deepak Chopra, just to name a few of my favorites, have extraordinary writings and wisdom on the subject of awakening and creating a happy life. I have read and reread many books on creating a better life, awakening, enlightenment, and general "self-help." What I have not ever come across is a book of that type that is just an easy, understandable read. I wanted to create a sort of guide written in layman's terms that anyone, at any point in their spiritual awakening can relate to. I want this to be as easy to understand as reading a recipe. My hope in writing this was to create a book that you can hand to a friend who needs to get out of a rut or needs a little encouragement.

Though this book is meant to offer additional tools and is not a substitute for professional mental care.

As I look back, I realize this path I have been on has been like a recipe. From time to time we have all received a recipe from a friend or found one on the internet that we want to try. The great thing about recipes is that you can add ingredients that will change the end product. Some ingredients will make the recipe worse. Some ingredients will leave you with a delicious result. I've had my share of bad ingredients. I eventually found some of the best ingredients that have brought beautiful results in my life. I want to share my recipe with you.

I have used the ingredients, or tools, in this book to create a very happy life for myself and find my true life purpose. My life experiences have thrown some pretty hard curve balls at me and prove that I've come through those trials a happy, healthy person, and each time a little wiser. I have suffered loss, violence, clinical depression, and attempted suicide along with various other hardships. I tell you this so you know that I'm not preaching to you from a pedestal. I have experienced enough trials and tribulations that my life certainly could have gone a totally different route. Through trial and error, lots of studies, and even more prayer, I am at a place in my life where I feel I can help others create a more enjoyable life for themselves. I have learned many things in my 50 years on this Earth that I wish someone had shared with me long ago. It would have saved me much heartache along the way.

Anyone can achieve and sustain a happy life. Unfortunately, some have never learned or realized they have the tools within themselves to just be happy and have the life of their dreams. What is more unfortunate is some have been taught things that work against that achievement. Sometimes it is even handed down from generation to generation like Great Aunt Martha's chipped porcelain gravy boat that you have sitting on a shelf somewhere because how can you get rid of it? It was handed down to you!

I would like you to think of this book as a guide. A guide to help you along the path of your spiritual awakening. I offer you ideas that you can insert into your daily life to achieve more happiness. Ideas that can help you clear out the stress and negativity that weigh you down. You are not necessarily going to agree with everything in it nor will you want to try every idea I give you. I just ask that you be open to what may be a new idea to you.

As you read, know that I am not coming from a place of ego. I am coming from the pureness of my heart to help you awaken to the reality that the life you want is already within you. You just have to clear a few cobwebs, adopt a few new habits, and let some old habits go. If you take away even one little nugget that helps make your life a tiny bit better or happier, then I have done exactly what I set out to do.

GLOSSARY

A glossary is usually at the end of a book but how silly is that? You learn the meaning of the words after you read the book? I noticed as I progressed down my path of spiritual awakening that I would come across certain words or phrases during my studies that I didn't quite understand. For you to understand where I am coming from when I use certain terms I'm going to "define" a few words for you with the definitions from my mind and my beliefs so that as you are reading this book, you will understand what I am speaking of when you come across them. We will discuss some of them more in-depth as we go, so don't get your feathers ruffled and stop reading if you see something here that you don't agree with. Remember, keep an open mind ;)

- <u>Aura</u>: An aura is an energetic field that surrounds every living thing. It is like a bubble that surrounds your body. Many people can actually see the aura of others. The ability to see auras is something that can be learned with practice. You can also *feel* someone's aura. It may come as a feeling of familiarity, untrusting, warmth, etc.

- <u>Awakening</u>: A shift in your awareness. You start to realize there is something greater in the universe, a higher power. You may feel hungry, starving actually to discover as much information about spirituality as possible.

- <u>Centered</u>: Think of being centered as how you feel when all is right in your world. When you can think clearly without any stress or anxiety. A place of calmness. You have a feeling of balance in your life. If you don't know what that feels like, read on. We are going to get you to that place.

- <u>Consciousness</u>: It is the energy and information that make you are aware of your existence. It is pure awareness. It is being; it is spirit.

- <u>Crystals</u>: Crystals are rocklike objects, mineral formations. They come in a multitude of sizes, shapes, and colors.

They can be used for many spiritual needs such as healing, protection, guidance, etc.

- <u>Ego</u>: Ego is a person's sense of self-esteem or self-importance.

- <u>Energy</u>: So I have to insert a funny story here to help you understand what it is I'm speaking of when I talk about energy. It is the entire reason for adding the glossary at the beginning of this book. I was at a conference some years ago, and they kept talking about the energy you were going to feel and experience. I was thinking that what they were referring to was the type of energy you get from drinking four cups of coffee in a short period of time. LOL at me. Turns out, everything and everyone is made up of energy. You can get to a place where you can attune to that energy. People can have good/positive energy. Or they can have bad/negative energy. For example, every time that one lady comes into the office you just feel uplifted because she has a great presence about her. She would be an example of *positive energy*. Or adversely, that guy who walks into the weekly meeting, and it's like a vortex opens sucking all of the life right out of the room. He would be an example of *negative energy*.

- <u>Enlightenment</u>: When we awaken to a level of awareness that we are one with everything in the universe, and we maintain that awareness all day and all night, every single day. We are in a place where we have pure love for every single thing.

- <u>God</u>: (*Warning: this one may be controversial,*) I believe that God is NOT an old man with a long white beard, sitting on a golden throne up in the clouds. I used to believe that when I was a child. I have come to know God, the Divine, the Infinite as the energy in everything and everyone. There will be much more to come on this subject you can be sure)

- <u>Grounding</u>: Grounding is an exercise that can be used to center yourself. To feel a connection with the Earth and the universe.

- <u>Higher Self</u>: Your higher self is your soul. When you hear that voice in your head, your higher self is not that voice, it is the one listening to that voice.

- <u>Intentions</u>: An intention is your plan or design that you set in your mind when you are trying to manifest something.

- <u>Intuition</u>: Simply put, a gut instinct. That feeling you get when you know something before you have any reason for knowing it.

- <u>Light</u>: Spiritually speaking light is joy, compassion, happiness. It is the overwhelming love of the Divine.

- <u>Lightworker</u>: A lightworker is someone who realizes their purpose on Earth is to teach, help, and guide others to find their purpose on Earth.

- <u>Manifesting</u>: Manifesting is intentionally creating what you want.

- <u>Meditation</u>: This IS NOT a religion. You may laugh if you know what meditation is, but believe you me, I am a meditation instructor, and sometimes when I say that to people who are, you know, uber-religious, they look at me like I have two heads. Simply put, meditation is a state of mind. It is a practice where you train your mind to go into stillness. It does not matter what religion you are or if you are religious at all, you can practice meditation.

- <u>Religion</u>: When I speak of religion as it is to me, I consider religion to be an organized system that has rules that you must follow to be a part of a particular group.

- <u>Spirit</u>: When I speak of spirit, I am speaking of one's soul.

- <u>Spirituality</u>: Not a religion. A personal practice to bring you more peace, to find your purpose, and to bring you closer to your spirit, your soul, higher self, and to God.

- <u>Synchronicities</u>: Coincidences that occur and appear to have meaning to something else. I like to think of them as messages from the universe that I am on the right track. For instance, during a meditation a few years ago it came to me that I am a branch. God is the tree. My flowers and beauty attract others to learn from me. And the pollen from my flowers will grow more flowers. After my meditation I picked up a book I had been reading and a few pages in, I saw this quote from the Bible: "I am the vine, you are the branches. He who abides in Me, and I in him, bears much fruit; for without Me you can do nothing." (John 15:5). Synchronicity? I think so.

- <u>Vibrations</u>: There are different levels of energy fields. Your energy vibrates on different levels. The higher your energetic vibration, the more attuned with your higher self, the universe, and source you will be.

1

MY JOURNEY

"Thousands of candles can be lighted from a single candle, and the life of the candle will not be shortened. Happiness never decreases by being shared." - Buddha

A new age is upon us. More and more people are waking up and realizing there is something more than the day-to-day, 9-to-5, rinse-and-repeat life that the majority of people are living. We are feeling a connection with the universe and realizing there is much more to this little life of ours. My spiritual awakening started many, many years ago, although I didn't recognize it at the time.

As it happens for many people, my spiritual awakening was spurred by a terrible time in my life. As a teenager, I went through a trauma that caused me to spiral into a hole so deep and so dark I didn't think there was any way to return. I suffered through this terrible time completely alone. I was too afraid to tell anyone. I kept a secret locked inside me for over 25 years. The event that occurred and the suffering in silence led me into a dark depression. I had been raped and I was so ashamed. I was honestly so petrified that I tried to just block it from my memory. I was so scared that if I told my parents, that my father would most likely kill the man who did it, and then my father would go to prison. I had to go on like it never happened. I couldn't let anyone suspect a thing. I wiped it right out of my mind. Or so I thought.

I became clinically depressed. I developed the eating disorder bulimia. My body started shrinking away. I wanted to shrink away and just disappear. Obviously, my parents and those around me noticed my physical changes. I guess they just thought this was some type of stage I was going through as a teenager. They did try to get me help for the eating disorder. I remember my parents taking me to see a therapist. Sitting in front of the therapist, I remember thinking to myself that this person has no idea how far away I am, and that there is nothing he or anyone can do to pull me out of this hole. I was right; nothing he said helped me. I couldn't bring myself to tell the therapist what happened to me. So of course he was not able to help me. He didn't know what I had been through. I kept slipping down that dark hole. Thinking about that hole to this day, it was a real place. It was like I was being weighed down and each day more and more weight was being added to keep me there. I slipped so far down that hole, I believed there was no way out. I decided I just wanted to go to sleep and never wake up. I took an entire bottle of sleeping pills. I went to sleep, and that should have been the end. At some point, I woke up and was violently ill. I then went back to sleep and slept for two straight days. When I woke up I couldn't understand how I wasn't gone. I literally felt like a failure. A failure because I wasn't successful in killing myself. I remember my mother yelling at me. She thought because I had been sleeping for two straight days that I must be on drugs. That is how good I was at hiding. Even my own parents didn't know that I had just tried to kill myself.

A few days later, I was sitting on my bed crying, which was a daily ritual at that point. A voice came into my ear and said, *If you want to be happy, just decide that you want to be happy.* The voice was so clear, and the statement was so simple. I didn't have to question who, what, why, when, or how. I just *knew.* I knew that whatever that voice was that spoke to me in that moment of brokenness was of a higher power. That moment, I dried my tears and said to myself "Enough is enough, I do not want to feel like this anymore. I want to be happy." And just like that, I was out of that dark hole and into the light.

I am not suggesting that it is easy for everyone to overcome such a tragedy. I know I was truly blessed. I was given a second chance at this life. I did have periods throughout the next 10 years where that dark shadow of depression would try to creep back in. I was determined to never go down that hole again. I knew that whoever, whatever, that voice was that spoke to me that dark day, did so for a reason. I believed that I had a purpose here. I was not on the path that was meant for me. I was meant for a path of happiness and light. I realized that I had tools to stay in the light and keep the dark shadow away. You have the same tools.

Over the years the darkness gave way completely to the light. The more light that came into my life, the more light I wanted in my life. The more I began to pay attention to the magical things happening around me and having gratitude for them, the more they happened. I began to realize there was so much more to this life than just being a wife, a mother, a good student, a great employee, etc. I was pulled to research and learn as much as I could. I read so many beautiful books. I went to conferences and retreats. I joined groups of like-minded individuals. I embarked on a path, seeking more light. As I began to learn how to bring more light into my life I desperately wanted to share that light with others. I cannot think of another term more perfectly suited to describe my path than a spiritual awakening. I have been on this journey my entire life, just like you. We start on this journey the day we are born. A journey that will take us back to our true self.

I believe that whisper in my ear that dark day, which nudged me into the light was a gift I am meant to share with the world. Every single person on this Earth can walk in the light. That is what we are meant to do. It is my sincere prayer that by sharing my story and sharing the ingredients, and tools that I have come to realize each of us possesses, it will help you to step further into the light.

These tools that each one of us already possesses are absolutely free and ready for you to start using today. You just have to start and then practice until it becomes a way of life. The individual journey we are all on has an absolute yet unknown expiration date, so why not live as happy as we can be along the way?

2

AWAKENING

"Awakening is not changing who you are, but discarding who you are not." - Deepak Chopra

The expression "awakening" is one of those buzzwords lately. You hear it quite a bit. Lots of people are talking about how they are *awakening*, *awake*; some are even *woke*. When a word becomes mainstream or it seems to be the latest fad word, I don't always have complete confidence that the user of that word actually gets its meaning. Rather, the user is just letting that word fall from their mouth because they heard someone they thought was cooler or smarter than them say it. It sort of devalues the word for me, but in this case, I don't care if it is the latest catchphrase or not. There isn't a better word for the experience that many people on our planet are going through than *awakening*.

For those who think they have not started the journey of their spiritual awakening, they will still notice that more and more they are seeing things in reference to awakening. They see the T-shirts, the memes, the cute coffee mugs that have cutesy little sayings on them. Those individuals may assume it is the latest society trend that will eventually fade away. They don't realize that we are all on the same journey: they just haven't found their way onto the path... yet.

Even though there appears to be a *trend* in our society of people awakening, it is much more than a *trend*. Hundreds of thousands have started this journey over the past decade. Many have been on the journey even longer. This *trend* is becoming a revolution in the spiritual world. If you are reading this book, I'm sure that you have started your spiritual awakening process. Whether you are just starting to wake up or you have been on the journey for some time, you will find some helpful tools here that will progress your spiritual awakening and hopefully add some clarity to what you are experiencing.

So exactly what is a spiritual awakening? What are we waking up to? First, let me tell you what you are waking up from. The majority of people go through their lives asleep. Have you ever gotten in your car, driven from your office to your home, pulled in the driveway, and thought to yourself, *"How did I even get home? I don't remember even going through any stoplights or anything."* I'm sure that you have had an experience like this. We humans go through life on autopilot. We are not aware of the world that is around us.

Awakening is a spiritual process in which a person begins to realize that they are part of a consciousness that is everything. You begin to wake up to the knowledge that there is more to our world, our existence, the universe, than you ever really considered. It is not a singular event. It does not happen in a moment or overnight. Awakening is a process. A journey. An evolution of you. The process may begin when you start to question things. Those questions turn into more questions, and soon you will get an answer or a little nugget that keeps you pushing forward for more. When you get an answer to one of your questions it is like a huge light just lit in your mind, and you are just blown away. It is an "aha moment." Literally one of my favorite things! Once you have one, you want another. Soon those questions turn into a craving for knowledge. You just know that there is something more to this life, and you want to find out more. Once your journey starts, there is no turning around; there is no stopping. You cannot un-know the things that you learn and experience on this journey. It is a beautiful path with exciting points of interest, enlightening moments of self-discovery, an expansion of your mind, and heart. It is a realization of oneness and an appreciation for life that brings a flood of joy to your soul. It is a feeling like nothing else you've ever experienced. You begin to see things in a way that you never thought of before. You feel as if you have been going through life thus far in a fog or asleep. Now, you're seeing things much more clearly. It feels as if you are awakening from that slumber that has been your life. You begin to remember who you really are.

You will start to judge time by B.A. and A.A. Your life Before Awakening and your life After Awakening. I think about myself B.A. and realize that people that I knew B.A. who have not been apart of my A.A. life, don't know the me that I am now. Not that I have changed. I have just shed away unnecessary layers that had built up over my life. I am now the true, authentic me. I have shed layers of a person that I carried around thinking was me, only to realize those layers that were built up over the course of my life were hiding the real me. I can barely remember that B.A. girl. I am constantly learning, growing, and it seems that with each level up I journey to, there is an infinite number of levels still to go. Yet the journey never gets tiring, rather it gets more exciting with each new lesson.

I cannot tell you how long the journey is or where the ultimate destination is because I am still on my journey. My guess is that this journey is going to last a lifetime. I can tell you that life A.A. is so much more significant, rewarding, joyful, and peaceful. I feel as if I have achieved great success in life. It is like needing prescription glasses and finally putting them on and looking through the lenses for the first time. Everything is so much clearer, so crisp, and defined. You never want to go back to seeing things the way they were before you put those glasses on. I believe that ultimate success is to realize and feel the pure love of God, source, or whatever you choose to call that divine energy. It is to not lose that knowledge and feeling when you are going about your daily routine with all of the noise and negativity of the world around you. It is a beautiful thing when that noise and negativity are so muffled by the joy in your heart that they just become a nothingness that has faded away into insignificance.

People around you will notice that you are different after you have started your spiritual awakening. They probably won't know what it is but they will notice. You might get compliments like, "You look great. Have you been on vacation? What have you been doing? You look so radiant." You may even be accused of having visited the plastic surgeon. It is because you are shining. You have light from within that radiates out to the world. Your peaceful demeanor will have others so intrigued that they will want to know what your secret sauce to life is. People will be attracted to your energy. They will enjoy your company because you radiate peace and love.

Awakening is not something that we can claim as an achievement. It is not something that we can claim we have accomplished. No trophy or participation ribbon is waiting for you at a finish line. Your spiritual awakening is a gift from God. It is right there for everyone. Every single one of us has the same size package, with the same wrapping paper, and precisely the same bow on top. Inside is the most glorious gift God could give you. But don't think that by getting to your package and unwrapping it before your neighbor or your friend that you did anything special or out of the ordinary. You certainly cannot claim this present as an accomplishment of your own. That would be your ego speaking, and you might have to have your gift set up on a shelf for a bit until you tell the old ego to go take a hike. Through the process of awakening, we begin to let go of ego. We will go into the ego in more detail in the chapter Leveling Up.

This gift of awakening isn't something that we open the box and poof, there it is. We aren't suddenly all-powerful, all-knowing superhumans ready to master the world. No, it is much more subtle than that. When you get to your gift you may be ready to tear into it like a wild five-year-old on Christmas morning, but it doesn't work that way. This gift unwraps itself. And let me tell you, it doesn't matter how hard you pull on that ribbon or pick at the tape on the edges, it is only going to open as fast as it wants to open. I speak from experience. I have tried to rush things along, and finally, I found the best tool you can have on this path was in me the entire time, though I never thought I had it. My path led me to patience. You will do yourself a favor if you find your patience as well.

The reason for the process is that if you were just handed the keys to the kingdom you wouldn't understand the real significance of what was just handed to you. To truly understand and have a deep appreciation, we need to follow the path. We need to take this journey through knowledge and spirituality because each step helps us to understand the next. I'm an avid reader and when my awakening started I wanted to consume all of the books I could on the subject. Sometimes I would pick up a book and not get what they were saying at all. Then six months or perhaps a year later, I'd pick up the same book and it would all make total sense. The reason for the change in my understanding is that I had now been on the path long enough. I had learned the lessons that I needed to help me to comprehend the subject matter in the book at this point.

That being said, there are some things you can do to further the process along and get some unwrapping done. There are tools and practices I will share with you that will help you to grow and understand the process. Right now you need to understand that this gift I'm talking about isn't like a light switch. It is not all at once. It is more like a dimmer switch. The light comes on but the further you go on your path, the brighter the light becomes.

This journey is about realizing who you really are. Read again the quote at the beginning of this chapter by Deepak Chopra "Awakening is not changing who you are, but discarding who you are not." On this path, there will be changes for sure, but you won't be changing *you*. You will be *remembering who you are*. You will come back to your true self. Your self that you will most likely not even remember ever existed. I know it all sounds really woo-woo, but I promise, the further you go on your journey the more it will make sense. Even after you have been on your journey awhile, you may still think it is all a little woo-woo. I have been on this journey for years, and I have just come to embrace the woo-woo. You will too, I'm sure.

One of the biggest questions I hear is "What about religion and God? Do you believe in those?" Here is my opinion on religion and God. Somewhere along the way, someone decided to put God in a box, and on the outside of the box they carved the word R E L I G I O N. You cannot put God in a box. God is not a one-size-fits-all kind of thing. God can be more than the Catholics or Baptists say, or God may be exactly what they say. We are not here to debate who or *what* God is. We are here to believe that *God is*. We do not have to be part of an organized group, aka religion, to have a connection with God.

I view God as a verb instead of a noun. God isn't some dude sitting on a throne in the middle of the clouds in a golden-gated community called heaven. No. That is not my version. I believe that God is energy. You do not need to wait until you get to heaven to introduce yourself to God. God is EVERYWHERE and in everything. You can introduce yourself to God right now. Take a walk, God will be all around you. In the flowers you see, in the sun that you feel on your skin, in the people that you meet on the street. When you get home, take a look in the mirror and you will see God there too. God is in all of us and everything around us.

We are one with God. There can be no separation between us and the Divine. You may forget this or you may not realize this but it is still true. You are the universe. God. I am that I am. Your heart beating inside you is just as much part of the universe as the trees and grass, the sun and the moon. It is all one.

If I haven't already, I'm about to ruffle some feathers here. Religion uses God as one of the biggest scapegoats of all time. You've heard the saying "It's God's will." No matter whoever or whatever God is to you, I'm sure it doesn't want bad for you. If God were to harm you, God would be harming itself. God's will is the most powerful thought put out to the universe. Religion wants to put the fear of God into you. Why would you fear God? Why would God want you to fear God? God is absolute love.

That absolute love is a love like no other. It is all-encompassing. I used to think that a mother's unconditional love is similar to God's love. I have always felt that no one could love either of my children as much as I love them. God does. God loves them even more. I realized after my awakening that I am not capable of giving the love that God has for us all. Even though I am a part of God, I am still just a spiritual being having a human experience.

Have you ever looked into the eyes of a newborn? Mom's and dad's especially, but anyone who has had the experience to look into the eyes of a newborn has seen it. That newborn has just come from the all-encompassing, unconditional love, and energy that we are all part of. That love, the energy is still fresh with the newborn. There has been no corruption from the world. That baby's love is as pure as anything ever could be. This is when you can catch a glimpse of what God's overwhelming love is. It is so powerful I can remember looking into the eyes of both of my newborn sons and feeling that powerful love like it was yesterday. I have just recently had the pleasure of looking into the eyes of my first grandchild. I can tell you those moments were moments of feeling Divine love.

Your spiritual awakening will help you realize how miraculous the love of God is. You will feel the beauty of it all around you. Your entire world will change. You will grow spiritually in ways that you never imagined. Your life will be filled with the magic of the universe. Life will make sense in ways that it never did before.

You will notice many things happening in yourself and your life as your spiritual awakening journey begins. The signs may be subtle at first but they will grow. Your awakening may begin like a seed that has been planted. The more attention and care that you give that seed the more it will grow. Look for these signs that you have started your awakening:

- Your actions begin to change for the better.
- Forgiveness comes more easily.
- You feel a connection with everything.
- Material items do not have as much significance to you as they once did.
- You have greater compassion.
- You are more attracted to nature.
- You are more turned off by negativity.
- You feel more joy.
- You feel more peace.
- You are seeing more synchronicities in your life.
- You have more gratitude for everything in your life.
- You enjoy your time alone.

- You pause and reflect more often rather than reacting quickly.
- You worry less.
- You don't feel the need to judge yourself or others.
- You are craving to know more and find your purpose.
- Your intuition grows.
- You become aware of bad habits and want to improve yourself.
- You have a desire to have more meaningful relationships.
- Relationships that are not helping you grow will fade away.

This journey of awakening is a beautiful process. Take your time. Enjoy every moment. When you recognize one of these signs, give thanks for it. Another will be right around the corner.

3

THE RIGHT INGREDIENTS: GOOD PRACTICES

"Spiritual practice is a daily cleansing. Negativity must be washed away if we wish to attract positive experiences in our life." - Sri Anandamayi Ma

I want to share with you some good practices, tools, and techniques. These are the right kind of ingredients to add to your spiritual recipe. If you use them they will help you on your spiritual awakening journey. It is important to understand that everything around you will have an impact on your journey, whether it is good or bad. We live in a universe where everyone and everything is energy. If you could see the energy with your eyes, I imagine it would look like tiny, multicolored dots all around every person, every animal, every object in our world. That energy has a vibration that you can feel inside your body. Other people can feel your vibration and you can feel other people's vibrations. You can also feel the vibration from an object. For example, I love crystals. In fact, I may be considered a bit of a crystal hoarder, but I don't judge. When I pick up certain crystals, I can feel their energy vibration. It is like electricity running into my hand and up my arm.

This vibration of energy runs continuously through your body, to the earth, to the chair you are sitting on, to the people in the room with you, and out your door to the trees in your front yard, to your neighbor walking his dog, to the clerk at the grocery store in the next town and so on. This vibration is the energy of the universe and is a continuous stream through every single thing in the universe. The stronger your energy is vibrating, the stronger your connection with the universe is. The stronger your connection is, the more you will receive signs, synchronicities, and the easier it will be to manifest the things you want in your life. When your vibration is high you will feel more joy, peace, and love. You will have more clarity. You won't be sad, depressed, or angry.

It is important to figure out what things or activities *raise* your vibration or *lower* your vibration. Raising your vibration is so important. When you learn how to raise your vibration, you learn how to change your life. The ability to raise your own vibration is like having your own magic wand. Let's take a look at things you can do to raise your vibration.

Spending Time in Nature:

"In every walk with nature one receives far more than he seeks." -
John Muir

Witnessing the beauty and creation of God firsthand has an automatic way of putting things into perspective. Your body needs natural light and air. Take off your shoes and plant your feet on the ground. Feel that natural connection that you have with the Earth. The Earth is a giant ball of energy with its very own vibrational frequency. When you tune into the Earth's good vibration, you tune out the negative vibrations around you.

Laughter:

"Laughter is the best medicine in the world." - Milton Berle

Have you ever tried to be sad and at the same time laugh so hard your belly hurts? It is impossible. Remember that saying, "Laughter is the best medicine." The more you laugh, the higher your vibration will be, and the happier your life will be. Super side benefit—laughter is contagious so you will be raising the vibration of those around you. We've all had that experience when someone is laughing so hard at something that we can't help but laugh too.

<u>Doing Things That Bring You Joy</u>:

"Joy is a net of love by which you can catch souls." - Mother Teresa

Think about what brings you joy. Is it spending time with your child, reading a good book, walking on the beach, or maybe cooking up a new recipe? Whatever brings joy into your heart will raise your vibration. Whenever I feel joy, I know that I am completely in touch at that moment with my higher self.

<u>Being Creative</u>:

"Creativity helps us find ourselves and lose ourselves at the same time." - Unknown

Do you like to draw or paint? Perhaps sew. Maybe you like to restore old cars. Anything that gets your creative juices flowing will raise your vibration at the same time. Creativity can also be a great form of meditation.

<u>Have a Good Morning Routine</u>:

"The breezes at dawn have secrets to tell you. Don't go back to sleep!" - Rumi

If you start the day off right, you will have a better chance of vibrating on high all day. I start my day off with a morning meditation and set my intentions for the day. I follow that up with some yoga and read something inspirational. Then I spend a little time writing. If I can get a little time in nature it just amplifies the vibrations for the day. Create a morning routine for yourself and stick with it. You deserve it.

<u>Eat Healthy</u>:

"Eat good. Feel Good." - Unknown

Eating food that is good for you is *good for you*. Do you know those prepackaged, man-made things that have no real nutritional value? Those are going to raise your cholesterol, not your vibration. If your goal is to raise your vibration you are ultimately trying to connect with your higher self and God. It makes sense, then, that eating God-made foods will raise your vibration. Head over to the farmers market for some fresh produce or even better, plant your own!

<u>Love</u>:

"All of the power of the universe is within you." - Ernest Holmes

Take a moment and focus on your heart center. Think about someone or something that you love. Feel that love and let it radiate from your heart center out through your body. Imagine that love radiating out to your family, your neighbors. Imagine that love touching hearts across the world. Love is the MOST powerful energy in the universe. Love IS the energy of the universe. It is our direct connection with God. God is love. We are love. Everything is made up of love.

Music:

"Music can change the world." - Beethoven

Music can shift your mood from a negative to a positive in moments. Feeling a little sad? Put on a cheery beat and let your vibration soar! There is high vibrational music that has frequencies that are created to raise your vibration. A simple YouTube search will get you dozens of examples to experiment with. Try different genres of music until you find the one that resonates with you.

Breath Work:

"Deep breaths are like little love notes to your body." - Unknown

Breathing techniques are scientifically proven to raise your vibration. Sit down and take a few deep breaths in through your nose and out through your mouth. Then imagine on your next inhale that you are breathing in all of the good energy around you. On your exhale, imagine any negative energy inside you being released from your body. There are numerous breathing techniques that you can research to help you raise your vibration.

Giving Back:

"No one has ever become poor by giving." - Anne Frank

When you choose to give back you are showing that you are grateful for what you have and you want to share. Random acts of kindness can raise your vibration. Pay for the person's coffee that is in line behind you. Volunteer, give to a charity, smile at strangers. Giving from your heart and expecting nothing in return is a beautiful thing. A great exercise that you can do is to mentally send love, health, and peace to the strangers walking down the street or sitting in the car next to you at the stoplight. They don't have to know you are doing it, just think in your mind and feel it in your heart that you are sending them love, health, and peace. It's a much better way to pass the time in a traffic jam rather than yelling at the person in front of you!

Forgiveness:

"An eye for an eye makes the whole world blind." - Gandhi

You may have heard the saying that not forgiving someone is like drinking rat poison and waiting for the rat to die. Holding on to things that others may have done to you is a poison to your system. If you learn to let go and forgive, you will rid your system of that poison that weighs your vibration down. Some of the best lessons we learn come from things that others have done to hurt us. Forgiveness applies to yourself as well. Start your forgiveness tour by forgiving yourself for anything that you've been holding onto.

Exercise:

"Exercise not only changes your body,. it changes your mind, your attitude, and your mood."

Take a walk, dance around the house, or take a bike ride. The more active you are, the more the energy will flow through your body. If you can do that exercise outdoors it is like a BOGO (buy one get one.) You get two for one: exercise and nature. You just leveled up on your vibration.

Self-Love:

"It's the beauty within us that makes it possible for us to recognize the beauty around us." - Henry David Thoreau

Showing yourself love is a great way to raise your vibration. Be good to yourself. Take an Epsom bath, get a pedicure, do something just for you. Don't be afraid to tell yourself I love you. I used to think that self-love was a conceited thing. One day I had one of my favorite "aha" moments when I realized that if I love God and I believe that God is in me, like I believe that God is in everything, then how can I not love myself? Think about it.

Say No:

"When you say 'yes' to others, make sure you aren't saying 'no' to yourself." - Paulo Coelho

If something drains your energy and you know it, it is okay to say no. All too often we do things that we know we'd rather say no to. You've probably had an experience where someone asks you for a favor that you really don't want to do. You say yes anyway. The entire time you're doing the favor, you're kicking yourself for not having said no. You must learn to say no to the things that you really want to say no to. This will bring more positive energy around you and increase your vibration.

Crystals:

"Crystals are living beings at the beginning of creation." - Nikola Tesla

Crystals are natural stones that come from Earth. Guess what they are full of? The Earth's natural energy. They have been used for thousands of years to raise the vibration and increase positive energy. Crystals come in all shapes, sizes, and colors. Each crystal has its own properties that can be used for a variety of things. Many healers use crystals. You can wear a crystal on your body or have them in your home. They are very often used as protection from negative energy. I find crystals very useful in helping with my mood. If I am not feeling the love at the moment, I will bring some rose quartz close to my heart and let it work its magic on me. Many people, myself included, can feel the energy of crystals radiate through their bodies. When I pick up a crystal and get a strong surge of energy from it, I know that I need whatever healing properties that crystal has to offer.

Gratitude:

"The Universe provides abundantly when you're in a state of gratefulness." - Dr. Wayne Dyer

I believe that gratitude is one of the most fulfilling practices you can have in your life. It also happens to be one of the most important tools you have to raise your vibration. I have had a daily practice of writing in a gratitude journal for almost 10 years. Each day I write out 10 things I am grateful for. Even on the days that I might be sad or stressed out, I write down my list of gratitude. I believe it is MOST important to practice gratitude on those days when you really aren't feeling that happy. Those are the days when we are evolving. I mean, when we are happy and living our best life it is easy to write down 10 things to be grateful for, right? But on those difficult days, when you still manage to sit down and find 10 things to be grateful for you will change your mindset. What if you had a lousy day? What if your pet passed today? You write down that you are grateful for the memories you have of your pet. You are grateful for the love you shared with your pet. What if your house burned down? You are grateful you still have your life. You are grateful you know you're learning something right now that will help you grow and evolve.

An attitude of gratitude will change the way you look at the world. You will have a glass half full rather than a glass half empty. You will raise your vibration. As you continue this practice daily, your vibration level won't drop off. Your attitude of gratitude will not go unnoticed and it will influence those around you. What a great thing to be able to write in your gratitude journal, "I am grateful my attitude of gratitude influences my friends to be more grateful in their life." As you send out this beautiful energy of gratitude daily to the universe, the universe will in return send you more to be grateful for. It is simple cause and effect. Karma. Karma doesn't have to have just a negative connotation. This attitude of gratitude will open your mind and heart.

You may be rolling your eyes, thinking that this lady is a little too chipper for me. Before you brush this practice off as silly, give it a try for one month. You can do it in the morning to start your day off with a grateful attitude. You can do it just before you go to bed as you reflect on your day. Just do it each day. Even if some days the only thing you can find to be grateful for is that you are still breathing or that you have indoor plumbing, write it down!

You will begin to notice that you find gratitude for things that you never really gave much thought to before. You will notice as you go about your days, you will spot things you want to write down in your gratitude journal. Let's face it, we take 17,000-30,000 breaths per day, and you only need 10 things to be grateful for? You have at least 17,000 right there. Try it at different times and just figure out what works best for you.

A list from my gratitude journal would look something like this:

1. I am grateful for God.
2. I am grateful for my family.
3. I am grateful for the guidance I am receiving.
4. I am grateful for the love flowing into my life.
5. I am grateful for the laughter I shared with my husband today.
6. I am grateful to see the joy and excitement in my granddaughter's eyes.
7. I am grateful for the beautiful meditation I experienced today.
8. I am grateful for the blessings I am receiving.
9. I am grateful I am healthy.
10. I am grateful I am helping others find their light.

Notice that I start every line off with *"I am."* That is because *"I am"* is the most powerful affirmation tool or mindset "trick" that you have. When you tell yourself *"I am,"* you are affirming that you already have that. Never write "I *will be* grateful when I help someone find their light." That is affirming that it has yet to happen and it is something that *I want* to happen. Go ahead and show gratitude as if it is already *IN* your life. Your mind will believe it and will bring it to your reality.

As you start introducing these good habits into your life and making them a routine, your vibration will rise. You will get a real feel for what vibrating on high feels like. After a while, you will realize which things work best for you to raise your vibration. Warning: High vibrations do become addictive. What a great habit to get hooked on!

4

A KEY INGREDIENT: MEDITATION

"Quiet the mind, and the soul will speak." - Ma Jaya Sati Bhagavati

An absolute key ingredient to a great spiritual recipe is meditation. There is no better way to raise your vibration than through meditation. Many studies prove all of the wonderful benefits of meditation. Your physical and mental health are tremendously benefited with a regular meditation practice. Even a brief meditation can calm your mood and help you get centered. When you meditate you are going within. You are quieting your mind to connect with your inner or higher self. Meditation is a purification process that enhances everything we do. When we meditate regularly, we start to bring the peace, silence, and calmness that we feel during meditation out into our daily life. You will notice that you are more centered; your thoughts are clearer, you are more present, and less reactive to situations.

You've most likely seen an image like this associated with meditation. I wonder what someone who is not aware of what the practice of meditation is about would think of an illustration like this. Do they think we are summoning aliens or something? There is no need to worry about summoning aliens; not everyone who is meditating is doing that! ;)

I joke, but there are a lot of misconceptions about meditation. Some people view it as something mystical or even bad. People fear things they do not understand. Another misconception about meditation is that it is somehow religious. Read carefully: Meditation is not a religious practice. No matter what religion you may, or may not be, you can practice meditation (and not feel guilty about it!). I get so many questions about meditation and religion. I was once asked how I could reconcile meditation and my belief in God. I was at a loss as to how to answer the question at the time. Today I answer that question like this: Meditation is not a religious practice. Many people of all sorts of religions practice meditation. Some people consider it a spiritual practice, which is what it is for me. But in its simplest definition, meditation is a mindful practice. I love the quote, "Praying is when you talk to God; meditation is when God talks to you."

Meditation also has tremendous health benefits. Studies have proven meditation can lower blood pressure and increase your immune system. It will reduce stress which causes you to have less anxiety. It increases the efficiency of oxygen in the blood. It improves metabolism and reduces the aging process. That last benefit alone sold you on starting a meditation practice, didn't it?

Meditation is from yoga which is the union of body, mind, soul, spirit, and environment. Meditation helps us bring our awareness from the busy world outside to the stillness that is within us all. When I mention yoga you probably picture exercise, stretching, maybe even wheatgrass, or for goodness' sake, goats! (In case you don't know, practicing yoga with goats has become "a thing.") While you aren't wrong in thinking of yoga as an exercise, there is so much more to it. Yoga originated in India, and it is a spiritual, mental, and body practice. The portion that was the physical exercise that we are more familiar with in the Western world was actually to keep the muscles and limbs of the yogis stretched and in good condition for their long meditation sessions. They may sit for hours upon hours in a meditative trance in the same position. You can see how a series of stretches before and after meditation would be necessary.

In the late nineteenth century and the early part of the twentieth century, yoga made its way westward but it changed from its original practices in the East. Yoga/ meditation practices did not become truly popularized in the United States until the 1960s. Even today, the mainstream probably does not understand the correlation between the two. But now you do, so you can help spread the word!

Being a meditation instructor, I have heard every reason why people think they cannot meditate. Let me tell you that if you can think a thought, you can meditate. The most popular reason I've heard is that they cannot stop their thoughts. Guess what? Neither can I. Nor can anyone else. Humans experience thousands of thoughts per day! And just because you are meditating doesn't mean that you have stopped those thoughts. Rather you learn to observe your thoughts from a neutral place. In meditation, you are not trying to control your thoughts. You are learning how to not let your thoughts control you.

Even though it seems our thoughts run together, and sometimes it seems like we have multiple thoughts at one time, that is not the case. There is an end of a thought and a gap before the next thought. That gap is so extremely small that you don't realize it is there. Through meditation and learning to observe your thoughts, that gap between thoughts begins to grow. It is the silence within us. In that silence is where we find our true self. In that silence is the magical place where we receive the guidance and the answers we search for. Once you experience the gap you will want to continue to visit.

I could fill a book on its own with the wonders and how to's of meditation, but here we are only spending a few pages. Just know that meditation is not as difficult as you may think. There are many different types of meditation. When I'm asked what the best meditation is, my answer is the one that you do. If you are just starting, I would suggest checking out guided meditations online or through the apps Insight Timer or Breathe. You will also find hundreds of great guided meditations on YouTube. One of the meditation styles that I teach is that of a mantra-based meditation. I think that people who are concerned with their thoughts taking over during their meditation will find the mantra-based style a great tool for them. It will help you stay centered on the mantra and your breath.

Before your meditation, you should make a list of your intentions. Go over that list just before you begin. You are going to set intentions, not expectations. Do not set expectations of the meditation. Do not try to force anything. Just breathe and relax. Each meditation is like a snowflake, they are all unique. They are unique not just to each person, but each person's meditation will be a different experience every time. When I am really blessed, I will receive great insight and know that I have visited that magical gap. Other times, I just have a quiet time with no guidance or great insights gained. Every time, I know that I am better off than I was before the meditation. It always centers me and gives me some peace even on the most hectic or stressful days.

Meditating twice per day is optimal, once in the morning and once in the evening. If you only have time for one, morning is the best time for your meditation. You will set yourself up for a successful, beautiful day if you start it out with the right mindset. It is good to have a designated spot to practice your meditation. It is a little mind trick. If each day you sit in a particular corner of your home on a particular chair and you have a meditation session, your mind will start to realize that, "Hey, when she is sitting here, it's quiet time." The mind will begin to automatically slow when you go to that space for your meditation. As a side benefit, there is a belief that the mat that yogis sit on for all of their meditations absorbs the wisdom that flows to them during their meditations. I think that is pretty cool! Imagine if you use the same cushion, chair, or mat for every meditation, and it is absorbing the peace that flows to you during your meditation.

You may feel like you don't have time for daily meditation. Do your best to find even a few minutes per day to meditate. I can tell you without hesitation that meditation will change your life. The results will be unmistakably clear to you.

This is where you will find your patience. This is where you will start to have greater joy and peace. Your mind will open like never before. If you want a fast pass on your awakening journey, meditation is it.

5

YOUR THOUGHTS, YOUR REALITY

"What we are today comes from our thoughts of yesterday and our present thoughts build our life of tomorrow: Our life is the creation of our mind." -Buddha

Our thoughts can be categorized into conscious and subconscious thoughts. Our conscious thoughts are those thoughts that we are aware of. Your conscious mind is responsible for your reasoning. For example, when you are doing a simple math equation you are using your conscious mind. Your conscious mind is responsible for the choices you make. Your subconscious mind is responsible for the actions you take that are involuntary. When you have an itch on your arm and you scratch it, that is using the subconscious mind. You do not have to think about the fact that your arm itches and you need to scratch it. You just scratch. Your subconscious mind is also where you store all of your memories and your beliefs.

While it is believed that the subconscious mind is more powerful than the conscious mind, the conscious mind can alter the subconscious mind. There have been studies that prove your conscious thoughts affect your subconscious. We need to be careful with our thoughts. You could be sabotaging yourself with your own thoughts without even realizing it.

The power of the subconscious mind may be difficult to grasp or accept. Remember though, we don't fully understand the workings of a cell phone or electricity or even how the sun rises and sets. We just know they do and accept it. Why not just accept that the power of the subconscious mind works? What is there to lose? Think of all there is to gain! Remember, everything in existence was first a thought in someone's mind.

Think about some of the silly things you say to yourself that you really don't mean. For instance, I have had a few instances similar to this: I have been searching for my reading glasses for the past 10 minutes only to realize they have been on top of my head the entire time. I say to myself, "I'm so stupid." Do I really think that I am stupid? No. Do I feel a little silly for spending 10 minutes looking for something that was on top of my head the entire time? Yes, but that silly error doesn't make me stupid. My subconscious mind, however, does not distinguish between the things I say to myself in jest and the things I say to myself in earnest.

One of the first things you need to do is start being nice to yourself. We are all our own worst critics. That is such a shame to say but it is a true statement. The voice in your head talks to you more than anyone else in your life. If you are like the majority of people on Earth, the chitter-chatter going on in your head is not the most uplifting. We tend to have a never-ending dialogue running in our minds. "I'm never going to get that promotion; I'm not smart enough; I can't, I'm not enough." Stop! Stop with the "I'm not" and the "I can'ts" because they are keeping you from your happiness. Negative thoughts are like weeds. Positive thoughts are like flowers. But as we know, weeds can take over a flowerbed.

People will say they are struggling with their thoughts or that they are fighting off the bad thoughts. Do you remember your mom telling you as a child not to ignore the bully in school? Your mind is a playground, and those negative thoughts are looking for a fight. Just ignore them. Acknowledge that they are there but do not participate in their argument.

We are usually the first to tell ourselves that we are incapable of something. Imagine you are in sales and had a great month last month. Your boss tells you she wants to see you double your last month. You immediately think to yourself "I can't do that." Well, with an attitude like that, you are correct. A great quote by Henry Ford is "Whether you think you can or think you can't... you're right." In other words, if you are telling yourself that you aren't capable of doing something or if you are telling yourself you are capable of doing something, your mind will believe either one, and your result will be what you tell your mind to believe.

Thoughts are self-talk. Thoughts are seeds. Seeds can grow a beautiful flower or they can grow a thorny cactus. The choice is what you choose to think. It is said, the average human has between 5,000 to perhaps 60,000 thoughts per day. At a bare minimum that's over 3 thoughts per minute if you count every minute in a 24 hour day. If you are only awake 15 hours per day that number increases to 18 thoughts per minute. I don't know about you, but I think when it comes to the number of thoughts I have per day, I'm probably an over achiever, and lean closer to the 60,000 range. What do you think is going to happen if the majority of the thoughts you are having are negative? You are planting all those seeds in there, and you are going to end up with a giant cactus growing out the top of your head!

Of course, you are not going to just turn off that spigot of negative thoughts pouring into your mind right this moment. But with practice, you can get that spigot down to a slow drip. You will eventually learn how to keep that spigot under control. You are going to acknowledge a negative or bad thought when you have one and then let it go. As soon as you hear it, realize that you just had a Negative-Nancy moment and let it slide right on by allowing a more positive thought to slide in. You need to let those negative thoughts go because if you dwell on negative thoughts, they will multiply.

Dwelling on negative thoughts is the fertilizer that helps them grow and spawn more negative thoughts. The more focused you become on that bad thought, and the more attention you give to it, the stronger it is going to become. When you ignore it, it just goes away. It takes practice. Each time you catch yourself and let it go, you are building a new habit. That is the habit that is going to bring you happiness. Even the happiest people you know have negative thoughts but they have learned how to let them pass by without causing any damage to their happy state.

While we cannot control every aspect of our thoughts, we can have some control over them. Our thoughts are one of the things in this world that we do have some control over. You can choose to only think and say good things about yourself to yourself. You can choose to stop worrying. You can stop thinking that you don't have what you want. You can start thinking about how grateful you are to have what you have. I think of the power of the subconscious mind as equaling what some refer to as the sixth sense. If you train your mind, it can be a very powerful tool.

If you could draw a timeline of your life with your thoughts on one side and on the other side the experiences you were having at that time in your life you would be able to see a direct correlation between your thoughts and your reality.

The following is an excellent daily practice if you would like to improve certain things in your life, like your self-confidence or your health. It can increase the love and compassion you have in your life. You can choose to do this each morning before you start your day or each evening just before you go to bed. Get yourself a notebook or journal and write out 10 things that you would like to be or have in your life. Start each off with "I am." For example:

1. I am happy.
2. I am loved.
3. I am confident.
4. I am joyful.
5. I am successful.
6. I am healthy.
7. I am compassionate.
8. I am attracting the friends I need in my life.
9. I am guided.

10. I am that I am.

I have done this almost every day for the past 8 years, and I promise you it has made a huge impact on me. I always write "I am that I am" at number 10. Think about that statement for a moment. It is a very true statement if you believe in the power of the subconscious mind. If you want to level up this exercise, write down a list of I ams and tape it next to your bathroom mirror. Each morning say the list out loud.

Another exercise is trying to "catch" yourself. Each time you "catch" yourself thinking a negative thought or saying making a negative statement, stop, take a breath, and turn that negative thought or statement into a positive one. If you catch yourself saying something like "I am so dumb," stop. Take a breath and say, "I am very smart, and I am grateful for it." After practice, it will come automatically. After even more practice, you will notice the negative thoughts and statements just about disappear altogether. It is just like training a muscle; you have to exercise it over and over again to get the results that you want. You will still have some negative thoughts, but you'll learn how to deal with them. Learning how to think is learning how to live.

I will leave you with this caveat to thoughts and producing a certain outcome that you desire. Always be sure that what you are thinking is for the highest and best good. Always be sure you are not thinking anything that would cause harm to anyone or anything. Then your mindful practice will provide you with all that you need.

For as he thinketh in his heart, so is he. - Proverbs 23:7

6

INGREDIENTS TO AVOID: BAD
PRACTICES

"If you do what you've always done, you'll get what you've always gotten." - Tony Robbins

Any good cook knows that the wrong ingredients can absolutely ruin a recipe. The following are practices you need to avoid to keep your vibe at a high level. As I talked about previously, there are many things you can do to raise your vibration, and there are also many things you can do to lower your vibration. It is important to realize and become aware of the things you might do that would lower your vibration, so you can avoid them. Some of the following are things many of us do without even realizing we are doing them. Some of them are habits we may have inherited from our family. They are just bad practices we can easily correct. All of them will certainly lower your vibration and attract bad energy to you.

Worry:

"Worrying is praying for what you don't want." - Bhagavan Das

That makes so much sense, doesn't it? Worrying is praying for what you don't want. If you believe in manifestation (if you are reading this book, I think you probably do) replace "praying for" with manifesting: *"Worrying is manifesting what you don't want."* When you worry, you are allowing your mind to take over and run wild with worst-case-scenario thoughts. You are rerunning these scenarios over and over in your head. You are imagining what it will be like when the worst thing happens. How you will feel, how it will hurt, how it will affect other people around you... Your imagination goes into overdrive. What do we do when we want to manifest something? (If you don't know the answer to that question, no worries; we will be discussing it a little later.) Simply answered: We *imagine* the thing or event that we want to happen. The better we are at creating that visual in our imagination the more likely it will manifest. Dwelling on worry brings results, so does concentrating on a dream. Which results would you prefer?

The best one-word description for worry is worst. Worry is one of the worst things we can do. Worrying is likely going to bring into fruition the exact thing that you are worried about. You are concentrating so much, putting so much thought and energy towards something you are so scared of happening. When thinking about a situation or waiting for an outcome, we all have thoughts about the worst-case scenario. If you dwell on bad, it will bring bad into your life.

Why not replace those thoughts with the best-case scenario?

<u>It's a Family Tradition</u>:

"Change your habits; change your life." - *Thomas Corley*

Sometimes low energy and negative attitudes are passed down from generation to generation like Aunt Martha's bone china tea set. Some families always seem to have the worst of luck. They always seem to struggle monetarily; they have health issues; they have relationship problems; they just seem to always get the short end of the stick. They announce every terrible event, bad luck story to anyone and everyone who will listen. They know the outcome of every event is going to be the worst possible outcome before it happens because that is "just how life is." What they don't realize is that by expecting the worst-case scenario, that is exactly what they are attracting into their life. If they would just turn their attitudes around, the energy flow around them would turn around. They would start to have good things happening in their life. I think the very worst part of this type of attitude is the children hear their parents, and those negative attitudes become embedded in the children's brains. The children grow up and have families of their own, and the pattern repeats.

It appears these type of people enjoy their demise in some masochistic way. To make things worse, they will even hold a grudge toward that underdog family member who somehow manages to break the cycle. You would think they would be happy that someone they love is living a better life than what they have had. But one of the traps they have let themselves fall into is they don't want anyone else to do better than they are. When we have that attitude, guess what happens? We hold ourselves back from getting any further in life. Remember, every action has a reaction. You wish ill on someone else, you reap what you sow. If you happen to know someone like this, run, don't walk, and take this book to them right now. Sit them down and start reading aloud to them (because they won't read it themselves; they like wallowing in their negativity). I know that the pattern can be broken. I believe people like this just don't know any better, and you can't know what you don't know.

The News:

"What you feed your mind determines your appetite." - *Tom Ziglar*

Once in awhile the news stations will try to put a "feel good" story on. Your local news may even have one of those segments daily. The problem is, you have to sit through all of the yuck to get to the good stuff. The reward at the end doesn't wash away the muddy energy you were just dragged through. Even if the news stories are about people on the other side of the world or about some sort of policies that really don't pertain to you, it still affects you. When you are listening to the muddy energy, even if you are letting it go in one ear and out the other, you are still going to get dirty.

What if you start your day off by having the morning news on while you get ready? Do you think that will affect you? Some studies show how watching negative news can have a bad effect on your mood. So if you start your day off with that negative drone coming out of your TV, you are setting the tone for the rest of your day. You have all this yucky energy on you that you take out of your house and into the rest of the world. You stop for coffee on the way to work and guess what? The cashier is having a bad day too and isn't exactly little Sally Sunshine which, in turn, makes you grumpy and rude back to her. You just spread your negative energy into the coffee shop and continued on to the office, where you are surely going to infect anyone else you encounter. Those infected are likely to carry the negative energy with them and infect people that they come in contact with. It is a toxicity that just keeps traveling and it all started because you had to flip that switch on the TV this morning.

OCD and Superstition:

"Superstition is the death of a thinking mind." - Dr. T.P.Chia

I used to be OCD and superstitious. In case you don't know what either is: OCD is Obsessive Compulsive Disorder. It is an anxiety disorder where your thoughts cause you to have certain thoughts that lead to behaviors that are repetitive and uncontrollable. For example, I used to have to vacuum the carpet in our house in a certain pattern. If it wasn't vacuumed in that pattern I felt something bad would happen. Superstition is when you believe that a certain action is automatically going to cause a particular reaction. For instance, if a black cat crosses your path, you are going to have bad luck. I feel like OCD and superstition are twins or at least sisters. Both things have to do with wanting control. Being OCD will disrupt your life and end up controlling the way you go about your daily life. Superstitions do not cause as much disruption in your life, but it is a slippery slope.

Superstitions have been around for centuries and are found everywhere in the world through various cultures. You may knock on wood, carry a rabbit's foot, throw spilled salt over your shoulder, or some other random act that was somewhere along the way programmed into your mind. Superstitions are handed down through generations. My mother would tell me not to do something out of a superstition that she had been taught by my grandmother and my grandmother had learned it from her mother and so on.

I used to expand my superstitions. The black cat crossing my path could apply to a squirrel that ran in front of me or a yellow lab or maybe a chicken crossing the road (okay, lame attempt at a joke there). If it were crossing my path, I wasn't taking any chances. I would mark an X on my windshield to ward off any bad juju those evil path-crossing pranksters were trying to send my way. One day I had one of my "aha" moments and it clicked for me that if I truly believe I can manifest the things that I want, well guess what? I can also manifest *the things that I don't want*! Well, that certainly sheds a whole new light on the situation. So, with this in mind, let's look at how a superstition could have actual visible results.

I'm driving along on my merry way, and that bad-luck black cat passes in front of me. I am driving, and I'm also on the phone, so I can't mark that X on the windshield. Oh no, I am sure I am going to experience some bad luck shortly because of that incident. I put the belief in my mind. I am throwing it out to the universe. To make matters worse, I am putting emotion with it because I have a sense of fear and dread thinking about what is going to happen. I have just conjured up a powerful spell to bring a little havoc to my life. If some sort of bad luck comes my way, I am going to *believe* that it was because I didn't put an X on my windshield. In all likelihood it wasn't because I didn't put an X on my windshield, it was because I *believed* bad luck was going to come to me since I didn't X my windshield. By the way, I should also get off the phone while driving ;)

<u>Jealousy</u>:

"The jealous are troublesome to others, but torment to themselves."
- William Penn

We have all experienced jealousy. Whether you were the one with the emotional feeling of jealousy or the object of someone else's jealousy. In either position, jealousy is not a good or comfortable emotion. Many relationships fall apart because one or both people in the relationship are jealous. This can be a romantic relationship, a friendship, or even a business partnership. Any type of relationship that involves two humans can be affected by jealousy.

Jealousy brings about feelings of fear, anger, resentment, insecurity, inadequacy, etc. It stirs up all of these toxic emotions and energy. When you are jealous you can easily create scenarios in your mind that are not true. Your jealousy will compound all of those toxic emotions to create destructive energy, which can tear a relationship to bits. Jealousy will wreak havoc on your relationships and your personal self.

You've probably heard the phrase "the green-eyed monster" used to describe a jealous person. That phrase most likely stemmed from green correlating with being ill or sick. Jealousy could be described as an illness. It will certainly bring about an unhealthy (or sick) relationship. A monster is not exactly a warm and fuzzy creature we want in our lives.

Rather than banning the green-eyed monster from our lives, let's learn to look at him differently. Sickness is not the only thing that comes to mind when we think of the color green. Green also represents growth, balance, and peace. The next time you feel that green-eyed monster start to surface, make a decision that you are going to use this experience to grow from. You are going to take a good honest look at the reason *why* the green-eyed monster is surfacing. By doing this, you can turn those jealous feelings into positive emotions. At the moment when you realize you are feeling jealous, pause, take a few deep breaths, and listen to yourself. Listen to your inner voice. Don't scold yourself for feeling jealous, just observe. What is it exactly that is making you feel jealous right now?

Perhaps you are jealous that a colleague at work received a promotion that you thought would be coming your way. You feel so upset. You are upset with that person for getting the promotion. You feel that they don't deserve it as much as you. They don't work as hard; they haven't been with the company as long. It just isn't fair! You're upset with your boss because she didn't *even think* of giving you the promotion! WTH! You even brought your boss a souvenir from your last trip. Well, she won't be getting another one, right?! You are even upset with yourself. You should have been working a little harder; you should have bought your boss a better souvenir!

Stop. Breathe. Listen. You hear all of those negative thoughts racing around in your head? Take one, just one of those thoughts, and try to flip it. Let's look at the statement that your colleague doesn't work as hard as you. Do you know this for certain? You may quickly answer yes, but *honestly*, how could you know this 100 percent? Is there a possibility that your colleague has done some overtime that you didn't know about? Could he have come in on some weekends to do extra? Even if there is only a remote possibility, there is still a possibility. Unless you have some way of knowing every single conversation and interaction that has gone on between your boss and your colleague, you cannot know why your boss felt that your colleague deserved the promotion over you.

Instead of having your little pity party with the green-eyed monster as the guest of honor, let's invite the green-eyed monster to a growth session. It is okay to wish that you had received a promotion instead of your colleague but you have to leave it at that. Recognize that feeling and then realize the right thing to do in this situation is to wish your colleague the best in his new position. Realize that for whatever reason, right now was not the time for you to be promoted. Perhaps you need to look a bit harder at how you have been performing at work. What could you have done better that would have set you up for that promotion? The universe is bringing to your life right now exactly what you *need* right now. It may not be exactly what you *want,* but it is exactly what you *need.* Now, you may be reading this, saying, "I am sick with a sore throat right now, how do I *need* this?" There is some lesson in your circumstance right at this moment, which you need to learn. That is as true as it gets.

If you want to promote good karma in your life, one of the quickest ways to do it is to wish good for others even when it is not the first instinct that comes to your mind. When in doubt, follow the Golden Rule. It works every time ;)

<u>Gossip:</u>

"Great minds discuss ideas. Average minds discuss events. Small minds discuss people." - Eleanor Roosevelt

I will tell you honestly that I used to get wrapped up in gossip. The latest news going around the office about so and so is often hard to ignore. The definition of gossip is "a casual conversation about other people, typically involving details that are not confirmed as being true." Yep, we all know that definition is true. We also all know that 9 times out of 10, the gossip going around is not all true. *Maybe* when the story was first started, there was a bit of truth to it. But as it passed from one person to the next, so much information was added or dropped that the story only has about one grain of truth to it by the time it reaches the fourth or fifth person.

Gossipers *want* you to engage in gossip with them. When you engage it makes the gossiper feel like it is okay to be gossiping. Gossip can be like a little escape from your own life. Maybe you aren't all that happy in your life and talking about someone else and their problems can make you feel a little better. In actuality, what you are doing is going to make your life even less happy. Maybe you gossip because you are bored. I'm sure you can find some activity that is going to be more beneficial to you than gossiping. Diving into gossip is like diving into a pool of oil. You come out with heavy residue all over you that weighs you down, and it is hard to wash off. When we gossip about others, we are harming ourselves as well as the person that we are gossiping about. We are sending out some very negative energy. It is a toxin being released that affects everyone involved. Every action has a result. If you send out negative energy, you are going to receive negative energy in return.

Beware of gossip disguised as a concern! You know that conversation that starts with "I wouldn't *normally* repeat this, but I just *really* feel *concerned*…" If a conversation is opening with a sentence like that it is a cover for this: "To make myself *not* look like a gossip, I'm going to *pretend* that the only reason I'm repeating something that I don't *actually* know to be true is that I have some grave concern for Marsha down the hall who I've never even had a conversation with and may not even recognize her if I saw her outside of the office." Did you just giggle at that or nod your head? You did, and it is because you *know* it is a true story that you've been a party to at some point in your life.

Some gossipers will hide their wrongdoing in plain sight. Those are the ones who start the conversation off with, "I don't mean to gossip, *but*…" In their mind, it makes what they are about to gossip about a lesser offense. In the South, we have a little saying that fixes anything that comes out of your mouth sideways about someone you really shouldn't have said anything about at all. That saying is "bless her/his heart." For example, "Marsha down the hall has really gained weight, bless her heart." In the Southern tradition, you just made it okay with those three little words, but you only made it okay in your mind. You can't make a wrong right.

Think about a few things the next time the chairman of the office gossip committee comes knocking at your door. How would you feel if it were you who were the subject of the gossip? Think about it for a minute. If someone is willing to gossip about someone else to you, don't you think that the gossiper would be willing to gossip about you with someone else? Believe me, they would and they do. What good are you doing by participating in the gossip? I guarantee you that you cannot tell me one good thing. Instead of spending five or ten minutes engaging in gossip, why not spend that time engaging in a conversation that brings you and the other party to the present, like sharing a silly story about your dog or your child? Maybe even a joke. Laughter is a great way to raise the energy in the room! Challenge yourself to not gossip for two weeks. You will notice that you will be having more positive, thought-provoking conversations. You will feel your energy vibrating at a higher level. You will most likely be surprised at just how good you feel.

You may lose a friend or two when you make the decision not to participate in gossip. If you tell a friend that you no longer want to engage in that activity they will either support you or they will move along with friends they can gossip with. Just remember that if you lose that friend because you are not willing to engage in gossip with him or her, that was not really a friend. That was someone who feeds on negativity. Congratulations to you!

Social Media:

"Less Scrolling, More Living." - Unknown

So I may not get many "likes" in this section but sometimes the truth hurts. We have become a society that spends more time interacting with people virtually than we do personally. A study was done in 2019 which found the average person spent 2 hours and 22 minutes PER day on social media! That is mind-blowing to me. That is an incredible amount of time. Of course that 2.22 hours per day on social media could be time well spent. We could choose to look at the world through rose-colored glasses here and believe that those 2.22 hours were spent on social media in uplifting conversations, reading positive threads from friends, etc. Instead, let's choose to be realistic. The average person spending 2.22 hours per day on social media is scrolling through reading the newest political arguments, the latest gruesome tales from the news feed, seeing the next drama unfold in the lives of "friends" that he or she may have never even met in person before.

We need to be more conscious that we are using social media. Also, we need to be more conscious of *when* we are using social media. We often pick up our phone, open the app, and start scrolling without even realizing we are doing it. It struck me one evening at a gas station just how much beauty I was letting pass me by while I had my nose stuck in my phone. I was sitting in the car while my husband filled the tank with gas. To pass that (what does it take to fill a gas tank—four minutes?) time, I opened my phone and started scrolling through my go-to social media app. I happened to glance up and realized that just beyond the gas station was the most incredible sunset. I put down my phone in that instant and took in the beauty of my world. Now when we stop at the gas station, I don't pick up my phone. Instead, I use that 4 minutes to observe my world around me and be present.

If you don't want to give up social media, have a plan for social media. Put your social media time on your schedule just like you schedule everything else in your day-to-day life. If you find yourself with an extra four minutes, don't immediately grab your phone. Stop and take in the world around you. Your social media feed will still be stuffed with all the drama and news when you get to it.

Rather than just scrolling through random postings, organize your social media. On Facebook, you could join groups that have interests that raise your vibration. Find groups with other people going through their spiritual awakening. On Instagram, you can sort out who you'd prefer to see in your feed. When you are using any social media platform it is very important to think about who you are "friends" with or who you "follow." If you are following a bunch of Negative Nancies, you need to find the "unfollow" button.

Fear:

"Never let fear decide your future." - Unknown

Imagine you are at the end of your life, looking back on how many things you didn't do because of fear. How deep is that regret going to be? You are out of time and your fear kept you from knowing if you could have been successful at this or that.

Cliché or not you have to live for today. We are here to LIVE. We are here to have experiences. Fear keeps you from living life to the fullest. Not fearful you say? Are you just playing it safe? You are going to your 9-to-5 job, putting in your time until it is ultimately time to retire but all the while thinking if you could just take the leap of faith and open that little business where you could work at something each day that makes your soul happy? But fear of failure wins out and you keep doing the same thing you've always done.

<u>Negative Energy</u>:

"Don't pollute your body by absorbing the negative energy around you." - Unknown

Negative energy will affect your health. There have been many studies done that prove negativity can cause high blood pressure, migraines, depression, anxiety, chronic pain, etc. I used to be in a workplace where the negative energy was so thick you could feel it when you walked in the door. I had chronic migraines. I had to take a prescription medication to try to prevent the migraines and even that didn't always work. Within weeks of leaving that job, the migraines stopped. No more medication is required. The cure was getting out of the negative environment.

When you rid your life of negative energy, your entire life changes. People around you with negative energy harm you, no matter how positive your energy is. As you become more awakened, you will find that those people suddenly find their way out of your life in a variety of different ways. If they are not helping you to grow, then they shouldn't be there.

An exercise you can do to be protected from negative energy is to ground and protect yourself. It is a simple exercise, and you should do it at least every morning. Simply imagine yourself connecting to the center of Earth. I imagine a sparkly purple rope (I love sparkles) around my waist extending down deep into the center of Earth. I also imagine roots growing from the bottom of my feet deep down into Earth. Next, I imagine a beautiful waterfall flowing over my head to wash away any negative energy that is in or around me. I send that energy back to the source with love. Then I picture a bubble of rose-colored light all around me that will act as a barrier to any negative energy that comes my way. If you've never heard of this or done it, I'm sure it may sound silly, but trust me, it works!

Eliminating the bad practices from your life is as important as adding good practices to your life. It may take a little time to eliminate them all. When they are eliminated, you will feel the upward shift in your vibration.

7

LEVELING UP

"Yesterday I was clever, so I wanted to change the world. Today I am wise, so I am changing myself." - *Rumi*

Becoming more aware of presence and ego are two practices that if applied to your daily life will help you to "level up" your spiritual awakening. While you may feel that you are already very present in your life, there are things you can do to take your presence to another level. The importance of being aware of the role your ego plays in your life and how you can overcome its need to be in charge may surprise you.

Presence:

"Nothing is more precious than being in the present moment. Fully alive, fully aware." - *Nhat Hanh*

One of the greatest gifts to yourself and even to those who you love is to learn to be present. Being present will lead to presence in your life. Having presence in your life is being aware and feeling the Divine within you and all around you. This is something that has slipped far away from us human beings in recent decades. I remember as a child being at family functions. Dinners at my grandparents' house, picnics, birthday parties, etc. We would eat, laugh, and play. We would have conversations and truly connect. Today there seems to be far less of these gatherings. When we do have them, everyone has cell phones out snapping pictures or taking videos. Some may feel the need to briefly take a peek at their email or texts. We are not fully present.

We need to put down the phones. Sure it is nice to have a photo to look back on. That's okay. Take a photo, then get back to the present moment. I guarantee that if you give yourself fully to those moments, the image in your memory will be even clearer than that picture on your phone. If you fully let yourself be present in the moment, later you will recall the sights, the sounds of laughter, the smell of the food, the joy and love you felt in those moments. Even the best camera out there can't capture all that.

If you have ever lost someone dear to you, you know how grateful you are to have spent time with that person when you were truly present. Or perhaps you know the pain of looking back on times spent with that person when you weren't truly present. Moments lost, never to be had again. You will never have regrets about being present in your life.

One of the awesome side effects of you becoming more present in life is that it will be contagious. I mean, think about it: if you are out to dinner with friends and you put down your phone to just enjoy the conversation and be present for the moments, do you think your friends are going to bury their noses in their phones? If they do, it's time to pick out some new friends. (Only half kidding there.)

As you practice being more present, you will discover presence. Presence is when you feel the Divine in everything you do. You recognize spirit in everything. You are aware of the higher power; God, your higher self, spirit… whatever name you want to put on it, you will feel it. It is joy deep within you. It is *knowing* that there is more. Knowing that you are connected.

Presence doesn't happen overnight. Being present is an exercise. And just like any other exercise, the more you practice it, the better you become. You will begin to catch yourself not *really* being in the moment. When you do, pause and take a breath in. Breathe in like you are breathing in your surroundings, and as you breathe out, let go of any of the thoughts or feelings that were keeping you from being present.

Another exercise that will increase your awareness in presence is to take a few minutes each day to really take in your surroundings through all of your five senses. For this example let's say you are sitting outside on a sunny day. Close your eyes. Take a few deep breaths in and out, feeling a bit more relaxed with each exhale. Feel the sun on your face, your skin, your whole body. Feel the sensation of soaking up that beautiful sunshine. As you melt into that sensation, give thanks for being able to feel this sensation. Now, focus on the sounds around you. Can you hear birds singing? Maybe the rustle of the leaves on the trees as the wind blows. Or perhaps you are in the city and can hear cars and other city noises. Listen. As you listen, give thanks that you have the ability to hear these sounds. Now, focus on the smells around you. Can you smell a fragrance in the air from flowers? Maybe it is the scent of fresh-cut grass. Whatever the scents are that fill your nose, become aware of them. Give thanks that you can smell them. The next may seem a little difficult, but what can you taste? Open your mouth and let the fresh air roll across your tongue. The taste of sunshine. If you live in the city you may be tasting car exhaust. But you get my point. Now, give thanks that you have the ability to taste. Finally, slowly open your eyes. Look at the beauty that surrounds you. Take it all in. Really look at everything within your sight. The magical blue of the sky, the white fluffy clouds up above. The different hues of green of the plants and trees. Give thanks that you have the ability to witness this beauty before you. With deep appreciation, witness all of it at the same time—what you feel, what you smell, what you hear, what you taste, and what you see. Realize the wonders of it all. Take it all into your heart, and feel your heart swell with the beauty of life that is all around you and inside you. Say thank you.

This practice is something that will profoundly change your life. Your gratitude will grow. Your love will expand. Your joy will radiate from your being. When we take the time to stop, be present and aware of our surroundings, the people, the animals, the world right in front of us, we start to notice it more. You won't be able to casually walk by a beautiful rosebush without realizing the beauty you are witnessing. It will resonate in your heart with gratitude. In response, the universe will send more beauty into your life. This newfound appreciation and presence will fill you up. The beauty of it all will build inside you, and you will beam with a glow of universal energy only capable of being produced by pure gratitude.

Ego:

"When the ego dies, the soul awakes." - Mahatma Gandhi

Let's talk about ego. Getting your ego in check will have a huge effect on the way you act and the way that you interpret other's actions. The ego is the route of many issues in our lives. Each and every one of us has an ego.

The "size" of one's ego will determine a lot about their life. What is the definition of ego? Ego is a person's sense of self-esteem or self-importance. In Latin, the word ego would translate as "I." I look at the ego as a part of myself that *considers itself* the true *I* of me. Keep in mind that I said "I *look at ego as…*" I do not believe that ego is the true I of me. Our true I is much more than the ego, and our ego doesn't want us to realize that. The ego wants to control. Whether it is my ego, your ego, or the little lady down the street's ego. Each one wants control of that *I* that they are in.

When your ego is in control of you, your actions are going to serve your ego. The ego is not acting to bring the highest and best good to you. The ego's MO is to remain in control. The ego wants to be fed, and its appetite cannot be filled. The more the ego is fed, the more ego wants to be fed. It is like a euphoric state where you don't even realize you have lost control to this soul-eating monster inside you. You may even feel a *high* when your ego is fed. On the flip side, an ego that is used to being fed regularly will try to cause you a lot of grief when it stops getting fed. But there are ways to curb that appetite without feeling the grief that ego tries to inflict. Ego takes everything personally. To the ego, it is the most important.

On your path of awakening, the ego will try to veer you off course at every opportunity. Remember the ego wants to control. When you are awakening and learning, feeling incredible new things, things that you never thought about before, your ego is going to fight it. What are signs that your ego is upset and trying to sabotage your awakening? Suppose you have started a meditation practice. You have decided that you are going to spend 30 minutes each morning meditating. When your practice first begins, your ego thinks that this is just the next *fad* thing you are following, and it will be over as quickly as it started. Kind of like when you start all those New Years' resolutions and then give up by mid-January.

As your meditation practice continues, you will start to see the benefits of meditation quickly. You stop being controlled by thoughts. Your reactions to things will be calmer, and you won't be so quick to judge. You will see this rather quickly and so will your ego. The ego will suddenly realize this is more than just a fad and that ego is starting to lose control. In an effort to sabotage your meditation practice, ego may get you to start thinking, *You know, this really isn't doing anything. I've just not had as much stress lately, and that is why I'm feeling calmer. It really doesn't have anything to do with meditating."* Or if you decided to commit 15 minutes each morning and 15 minutes each evening but you wake up a few minutes late in the morning, your ego will try to convince you to just skip that morning meditation. Evening rolls around;

you're tired; you'd like to just crash in front of the TV, but you have a meditation to do. The ego will work on you to just skip it; you can double up tomorrow. And so on. Beware. Your ego is trying to fool you because it knows it is starting to lose control.

The key to avoiding the trickery of the ego is to be aware. Awareness is the key to everything on this path of awakening. If you are aware when that thought comes in and says, *Just skip this morning's meditation,* you will know that ego is losing control; therefore, you are on the right path. Kudos to you! I always get excited when I recognize the ego's little mind games because that is when *I know* for sure I am on the right path.

The more you become aware and don't let ego get away with veering you off course, the more your true self, your true *I,* is present. When you notice this about yourself, you will feel very proud of yourself. No worries, this pride is not that of ego, it is more like joy. You will feel pride and joy that you are tapping into your authentic being.

The more you become aware of the ego and how it works, the more you will see how the ego is working in other people's lives. I have had a successful career in sales. Let me tell you, there are some HUGE egos in the profession of sales! I was once very competitive. That competitive nature was the fuel for my ego. Somewhere along my awakening journey, I realized how little it meant to me to be recognized for top sales for the month or whatever award was being given out. I realized those things were not what defined me. My ego may have disagreed, but I knew the truth. After sitting back and taking a genuine look at my priorities, I came to the conclusion that as long as I was making the income that I needed to help support my family, those ego-fueling awards really had no great importance in my life.

You will know when you are getting free from your ego. When you start to feel you don't have to make any sort of impression on anyone. When you don't measure yourself with anyone else. You are being you. Getting rid of the ego is like a butterfly coming out of the cocoon. You will transform and be something so much more beautiful. You will not miss that ego. You will feel free to be present in all areas of your life without any inhibitions.

Your newfound appreciation for being present along with learning how to stop your ego from controlling you will level you up on your path of spiritual awakening. These two things will have a huge impact on you. You will be filled with light. Your true self will step out into the world.

A note of caution. Don't become a "spiritual snob." You may feel you are rising above the negativity of the world. You aren't letting your ego control you like other people let theirs control them. None of that means that you are "better" than anyone else. You have been blessed to have your eyes, and heart open a little faster, or a little more than others you know. Be grateful. Say a prayer that all the people in the world will open their eyes and hearts to let the light flow in.

8

TEN SIMPLE TIPS TO QUICKLY CHANGE YOUR MINDSET

"We cannot solve our problems with the same thinking we used when we created them." - Albert Einstein

I want to put all of the tidbits that have clicked for me in one place so hopefully, you will find something that will click for you too. Dog-ear this chapter; put a pin in it, a bookmark, or whatever will help you find it quickly when the time comes. If you find that your thoughts are veering off course, and you need a nudge in the right direction, head to this section. Here are my special ingredients. The ideas, practices, and quotes that have helped me along the way:

1. <u>Reading Quotes to Pull You Out of a Negative State</u>: This one is so easy, and it works every time. There was an occasion where I was upset about something or other and was searching Google for just the right quote to express my mood. I noticed that when I was searching, many of the quotes were opposite of what I was feeling. I

kept reading. After a few minutes, I realized my mindset had shifted, and I was feeling much better.

The next time you need a change in your mindset, try this exercise. Type the opposite of whatever ails you into Google, add "quote" to the end, and hit "images." So if you're sad about something, type in "happy quotes." You will get all sorts of ready-made images with quotes. Read those quotes until whatever was upsetting you has settled itself. It may only take reading two or three quotes, or it may take reading 20. At some point, you will start feeling better. With the search a quote, read a quote method, you can change your mindset in minutes. You will realize that your thoughts had been twisted around whatever emotion that you were Googling and by replacing those thoughts with others, you changed your mindset.

Side note: When you are searching for just the right quote to counteract whatever negative mindset you are in at the moment, make sure you save it. The next time you are feeling the way that you are now you can go back and read it again. Or because you took the time to read it and save it this time, the next time you are feeling that way, you may just recall that quote and move on.

2. <u>No More Mind Reading</u>: Stop thinking that you can read someone's mind or that they can read yours. If

you or they were truly psychic, you'd both know there are ground rules that must be adhered to by psychics, and one of them is that they do not read other's thoughts without that person's permission first. FYI.

You aren't really mind reading at all, are you? You are actually assuming. You are assuming that someone thinks this way or feels that way. You are projecting your thoughts and feelings onto that person. Not to be sexist, but we ladies are masters at this. Perhaps it is because we have such great intuition. That intuition causes us to feel that we can know what another person is thinking. We can certainly get caught up in it. I know I used to be convinced that I knew how someone else felt about me until an occasion occurred where I actually sat down with the other person to discuss my thoughts and feelings.

During that conversation, I told that person that I felt sad, hurt, and neglected by her. Over the previous few months we hadn't talked very much and she seemed to be spending a lot of time with someone I had issues with previously and no longer associated with. I *assumed* she had developed this great friendship with this other person and no longer had space in her life for me. She had no idea that I had been feeling that way. Not one clue! Why would she? I hadn't told her unit now. As she sat back and listened to what I was telling her, she realized how I could have taken things that way but in reality, nothing that I had assumed had been correct. The time she had been spending with the other person was strictly for a business project. She had been consumed with her business for the past few months, which gave her no time to socialize with anyone. After recounting the previous months, she realized the time had gone by so quickly and that she was so busy, she had neglected not only our friendship but several others as well. My assumptions had been completely wrong. My assumptions caused me to have an unnecessary feeling of upset. My assumptions caused me to suffer from a negative mindset.

I learned a big lesson that day. No more mind reading. Which in reality meant, no more assuming. I had assumed I knew what my friend was thinking. I assumed to know how she felt about me. Those assumptions caused me to have certain feelings. I let those feelings build up inside me. Those assumptions made me sad. Had I not just assumed, and instead, went to talk with my friend to ask her questions about the situation I wouldn't have gone through this sadness. I had myself all worked up over nothing at all. I made a promise to myself that day to never assume anything again.

3. Take it With a Grain of Salt: Unfortunately in today's world, we hear a lot of untruths. From news, social media, people in general fluffing up their stories to sound more exciting or more devastating. We are getting

misinformation all over the place. Do not assume that everything you hear, see, or read is true. (There's that "assuming" lesson again.) Be a listener. Be an observer. My dad used to say, "Take it with a grain of salt," meaning accept what you are hearing but know that all of what you are hearing may or may not be the truth. This may seem like a skeptical way to view the world, but it is a way that will keep you from making assumptions that may hurt you.

4. <u>Be an Observer Not a Reactor</u>: When a problem comes up, just observe it. Take a breath and really take a look at the issue without giving into a quick reaction. Do not get tangled up in the problem. If you recognize there is a situation and observe it as if you are a bystander, you are going to find a solution much more easily. The best practice when a problem arises is to pause, take a few deep breaths in and out. This will keep you in a calm mindset.

5. <u>Change Your Surroundings</u>: To quickly change your mindset, take a break from where you are. Take a short walk outside; take a shower. Even walking into another room can help. If you are feeling a low vibe, or you aren't feeling centered, you need to make a change. Start by changing where you are at the moment.

6. <u>People</u>: Have you ever heard that you are the average of your five closest friends? I don't take that for

an absolute but it does remind me that we start to take on characteristics and mentalities of the people we are around the most. Sometimes we have people in our lives that we love, but they are Negative Nancies. You need to take a break from them or at least learn how to put yourself in a protective bubble so you don't absorb their energy. Find a tribe to raise your vibe. Look for friends who raise your vibration through positive and inspiring conversations and activities.

7. <u>Help Someone</u>: If you want to change your current attitude, help someone else change theirs. Think about when you are checking out at the grocery store, and the clerk is a little less than friendly. Take notice of something she may be wearing, like a bracelet, and compliment her on it. On one occasion when I did this, the previously grumpy clerk began to beam over the compliment I had given her on her bracelet. She told me how her son had purchased that bracelet for her. She told me that she doesn't see him often, but it is a great reminder of him for her. I made her feel good, and I felt good for knowing that I perked up her mood.

8. <u>Music</u>: We talked about how music will raise your vibration, but it deserves a second mention. I'm sure you realize how quickly music can change your mood. If not, the next time you are feeling a little lazy or bored, turn on some upbeat music, and just see if you can keep your toes

and fingers from tapping! Music raises our vibration quickly.

9. <u>Gratitude Will Change Your Attitude</u>:
My favorite. Grab your gratitude journal and put pen to paper. What touched your heart today? Tell the universe what you are grateful for this moment. If you need a refresher, check out the section on gratitude in The Right Ingredients: Good Practices.

10. <u>Meditation</u>: Meditation helps calm you. You begin to feel a feeling of inner peace. Expanding your peace and calmness helps energy flow through you. That peace and calmness will act as a positive energy magnet. Meditation also increases your awareness. When you become more aware of your higher self, you begin to sustain a higher vibration. Even a brief meditation will change your mindset for the better.

The key to changing your mindset is to *recognize* that it needs to be changed. We tend to let our emotions steer us wherever they want us to go. With practice, over time you will become more aware of your emotions. You will recognize when you need to adjust your mindset. The simple tips in this chapter will help you. They will become second nature after some practice.

9

YOUR MAGICAL SELF
HOW TO CREATE THE RECIPE OF THE
LIFE YOU DESIRE

"What you think you create; what you feel you attract; what you imagine you become." - Unknown

The further you go on your spiritual awakening path, the more you will come to see how powerful your mind is. Once we learn that we have our higher self, spirit guides, God, and a whole universe that is helping us along this life path, we begin to realize that anything is possible. We learn that we are basically magical beings. The definition of magic is the power of apparently influencing the course of events by using mysterious or supernatural forces. Using our thoughts to create or manifest the life we want, the things that we desire is like magic. We are influencing the course of events by using what most humans would consider a mysterious force.

With the right tools and practices, you can begin to manifest the life of your dreams. There is much more to manifesting than just taking a clipping from a magazine and pinning it to a vision board. While vision boards are great, and I always have one too, a vision board without setting a specific intention is just a board with pictures to remind you of your dream life. You may end up with an item or two that were on your vision board, but if you learn how to really put an intention behind your vision board or desire, then you will have a much higher success rate.

Simply defined, an intention is a plan. So essentially when we are setting our intention for something that we want to manifest into our life, we are laying out a plan. We create a design. Great businesses or communities always begin with a design or plan, an intention. When you want to manifest something into your life, be it money, career, love, new home, etc., you need to have a clear intention. Your intention is your beginning.

As adults, we forget a very valuable tool that we used all of the time as children. As we go from childhood to teenage years, we want to grow up, become an adult, so we try to separate ourselves from anything childlike. Our imagination takes its first big hits during this time. We stop pretending. We no longer do that wonderful thing we did as children where we were what we imagined. Remember when you were playing as a child and using your imagination? As a child, there were no limits on your imagination. With a few blankets and a bunk bed, you could imagine you were on a pirate ship in the middle of the ocean. I had a very vivid and creative imagination as a child. We had a little wooded area with a creek running through it behind my childhood home. I used to take my Barbies and their camper down to the creek. I'd park it alongside the edge of the trickling water and set up "camp" for the Barbies. I would imagine that they were at a grand park with river rapids streaming by them. I used my imagination to alter the small wooded area around me into a lush forest where the Barbies would go on vacation. When setting an intention for manifesting, you need to tap into that inner child and use that childlike imagination. There are no limitations.

Let's use an example that you are trying to manifest a new love into your life. Close your eyes, and imagine what that person would be like. What color are her hair and her eyes? How tall is she? Does she smile a lot? What does her voice sound like? What does her laugh sound like? Picture her in your mind, and picture how she sounds. Does she wear perfume? Can you smell her lovely scent? How does she make you feel? Where do you go together? Imagine the things that you will do together, the places you will see. *Feel* the love in your heart for this beautiful person in your life. *Feel* your heart swell with love and gratitude that you now have a partner to share things with on this life journey. The more creative you can be with your imagination, and the stronger you can *feel* the love and gratitude, the better.

Now with that clear intention set in your mind's eye, release it out to the universe. *Know* that it is done. Don't wish for it to be done. Don't hope for it to be done. Don't think that it will be done. KNOW that it IS done. Imagine all you can about what you are manifesting. See it, feel it, smell it, hear it. Feel like it is here and done. Do not imagine the process of *how* what you are manifesting will happen. It is not our job to figure out the *how;* it is our job to picture the end result. The universe will take care of the *how,* and we must trust that.

Do not attach negativity to something by accident. Don't walk around all day wishing for what you are manifesting. Don't think about how much you want what you are manifesting. If you are thinking of it in terms of want, what does that say to your subconscious? It says that you don't have it. We need to be telling our subconscious that we already have it. Our subconscious will in turn work out the details along with the universe and bring to fruition that which we are manifesting.

As adults, the part of our imagination that we still use is being used for bad instead of good. Imagining worst-case scenarios. If our imagination can bring about our dreams, it can also bring about our nightmares. You've heard the saying "I can't even imagine." Can you *imagine* how many people said that to Edison when he told them his idea to create a light bulb? They were right; they couldn't imagine. But Edison could and he did.

Decide to wire in the future identity of yourself right now? Think about where you would like to be five years from now. What would you look like? How would you be dressed? Where would you live? What would your home smell like? What would it sound like outside your home? Picture it all in your mind. Imagine exactly how you would feel standing in the kitchen of your home five years from now knowing that you have accomplished everything that you wanted to accomplish. Now go about the rest of your day feeling as if you already are your future self. Don't think *I want to be like this in five years.* Think to yourself that you already ARE that self.

Setting your intention at the end of meditation is a powerful technique. When we meditate we are slipping into that gap where our subconscious or our higher self is. The gap or the silence within teaches us who we really are. It leads us back to being our true selves. I see our higher selves as quite magical. After meditation and returning from the gap, we can set our intention. It is like you are planting a seed in freshly tended-to soil. Once the seed is planted, leave it there, and let nature take its course. Trust that the universe now has this seed in its hands and will deliver to you that which you desire to be manifested. Don't let any thoughts to the contrary enter your mind.

Another great time to set your intention is in the early hours of the morning. Even though I'm far from a morning person, I've always felt that there is something magical in the air of the early morning just before the sun rises. Generally, there is less activity going on around your house, your neighborhood, your city in the wee hours of the morning. If there are fewer people up and about, there is less energy flowing around. If you are sending out this intention through your mindful energy, there is less gook for your intention to make its way through to get out to the universe. If you do this practice at another time of the day like 5 p.m. you are competing with much more energy. That's the time when most people are rushing home from a long day of work; they are in rush hour traffic honking, and beeping. The energy in the area at that time of day is thick at that point and probably not the most positive. If you are sending out your intention to the universe at 5 p.m., that intention is going to have to work its way through a lot more energy than at 5 a.m.

Don't forget gratitude. Gratitude is so important on so many levels, and it is a key ingredient to manifestation. When we show gratitude, we are acknowledging a higher source. It shows our belief and trust. It also shows that we know we are just a cog in this life machine. When you see things manifesting into your life, show true gratitude. Even little things. Show gratitude. The more you notice manifestation in your life and the more gratitude you show, you will begin to notice more and more things showing up. Don't be hesitant to try to manifest for others. As long as it is for their highest and best good.

While gratitude is a key ingredient, love is the core ingredient in this recipe. The energy vibrating through the universe that creates all is love. Manifesting from a place of love is key. When you are setting your intention, feel the love in your heart center. Let that love radiate out into the universe. Let it build up so big that it is spilling out of you. Think of all the things that bring you love. Feel the love you will have for that which you are manifesting. If you are coming from a place of love, you are on the right path.

Remember, we are spiritual beings having a human experience. We have unlimited access to the magic of the universe. Through our minds, we can reconnect with our higher self. Our higher self loves us unconditionally and will assist us in manifesting.

10

LIFE CHANGES ON THIS PATH

"When things change inside you, things change around you." -
Unknown

As you go through your spiritual awakening, there are going to be many changes on many levels. Many are inward, but there are also outward changes. You may experience people being removed from your life. This happened to me on several occasions. It actually continues to happen to this day. The expression "People come into your life for a season, a reason or a lifetime" is a great way to think about the end of relationships. I believe that if we are not learning and growing from having a certain person in our life, the universe just guides us on a path away from that person.

As I look back over my life, I see the people who have come and gone. I know what lessons they were there to teach me and why they are no longer a part of my life. As I progressed further into my spiritual awakening, there were a few friends I knew who didn't give any credit to the things I was starting to believe. I had a few who would actually make fun of me. I was never offended by that or felt attacked. I knew that sometimes you just can't understand what you don't understand. It wasn't my place to try to push my beliefs on them, not that that would work anyway. When some of those friendships ended, it truly saddened me but ultimately I knew why. I knew they were removed from my life because I needed to continue on my path. I needed to do more growing. These particular friends were holding me back from that. The loss of some of these friendships was gradual; some were sudden. In hindsight, they all began and ended at just the right time.

The part of the earlier quote about people coming into your life for a lifetime, I have those people too. I am more grateful to those people than I can express. I want to point out here that your "season, reason, or lifetime" people are not necessarily just "friends." We are also talking about family. Many of us (probably all of us) have family members in which the only thing that we have in common is blood. Just because someone is a family member doesn't mean that you must have a relationship with them. Remember that it is okay to walk away from a relationship that no longer serves your highest and best good. Even if that relationship is with someone you are related to.

It's important to know that when someone is removed from your life, whether it is via a terrible fight, or that they move away and you lose contact with them, there is a reason. There could be a variety of reasons. The one thing that is a constant, no matter how they leave, is that you should take the time to go inward and thank the universe for the lessons you learned from this person. Even if you don't see what that lesson is at the moment. Pray for that person to have the highest and best on their journey.

A good practice when a relationship has come to an end in your life is Ho'oponopono. Ho'oponopono is a Hawaiian practice of forgiveness. Simply described, you think of the person whom you need to reconcile feelings for and say, "I love you. I'm sorry. Please forgive me. Thank you." This practice can have a powerful effect on you. When we have had a relationship of any type with someone, we have been in each other's energy fields. Our energies have combined, if you will. If we want to cut ties with someone, we need to make sure that we cut off their energy from ours. This is commonly referred to as "cutting the cord." Ho'oponopono can help you to cut the cord.

You can also have someone help you to cut the cord. A healer can perform a ceremony that will cut the cord of energy that connects you with another person or persons.

You can actually feel an immediate release like a giant weight has been lifted from you when you have a cord-cutting.

It is important to point out that while we will have friends and family members in our lives that don't *get* our path of awakening, remember you are a lightworker. A person may tease you about one of your beliefs today, but six months, or even five years from now, that thing they were teasing you about may click in their mind. They may think about it and finally understand what you were talking about. You may never have contact with them again, and you may never know this. All of us on this path of spiritual awakening, no matter where you are on your journey, are planting seeds all along the way. Those seeds are in the minds and hearts of every person we come in contact with in one way or another.

Our path of spiritual awakening is not always an easy one. But every twist and turn, every obstacle in our path that we have to endure or overcome is part of the process. As you progress further and further down your path of spiritual awakening you will look back on those obstacles and realize there was a valuable lesson in each one of them. Those lessons helped you progress further along the path. Find the value in every little thing in your life, give gratitude to it, and you will be blessed.

One of the most fun changes on this new path for me are synchronicities. If you listen and watch closely, you will be given signs that you are on the right path once you start your journey of spiritual awakening. These are commonly referred to as synchronicities. Not to be confused with a coincidence. A coincidence is when something happens by chance or luck. A synchronicity is when there is a meaning behind that coincidence. Examples of synchronicities are:

- You are thinking of someone and they call or you run into them shortly after your thought.
- Being in the right place at the right time.
- Seeing reoccurring numbers like 11:11, 2:22, 4:44.
- You think of something and it comes into your life. For example, you were thinking of an old song you like and you turn on the radio and it is playing.

These little magical moments are the universe's way of telling you that you are on the right path. Whatever you are doing is leading you to where you need to go. You will start to see more and more the longer you are on your journey. The closer you stay on your path, they will begin to pop up everywhere. You won't be able to keep a smile from curling up on your lips or to suppress that childlike giggle you have when you see one after the next nudging you along.

Eventually, the magical moments will grow into larger synchronicities. I like to call them God-winks. They are like little inside jokes between you and the universe. Each time I experience a God-wink, I acknowledge it and say thank you. The more you acknowledge them and give thanks for them, the more God-winks you will receive. Feel the joy each time you experience synchronicity because the universe has just winked at you. What could be more joyful than that? When you receive a God-wink, after saying thank you, ask for more guidance. Ask if to be told if this sign has a significance that you need to realize. Always ask for guidance. All knowledge is already in you. You just have to reach out and connect with your higher self.

I was once in a position where I wanted a major shift in my career, but I could see no way of that happening. I felt totally stuck. I went for what was supposed to be a quick lunch with a couple of friends. As we chatted, the conversation quickly turned to my career, and I told them how I felt. I explained to them how unhappy I was at my job. To my amazement, they were very encouraging and told me it would be the best thing for me to make this change. They told me how they could see that my current situation was a huge drag on me. This quick lunch conversation turned into a two-hour "intervention" as I like to call it. I made a decision that afternoon that I absolutely wanted to make this change. I had no idea how it was going to happen. I just put it out to the universe and let it go. I imagined my new position and felt myself sitting at my new desk in my new office and just trusted that it would happen. Exactly 40 days from that conversation, that shift in my career happened without me doing anything to force it. It just happened.

If you'd like another example of synchronicity in my life, I had one happen while writing this chapter. I pulled up my calendar to count the number of days the shift I just mentioned took. I realized exactly four years prior to the day I'm writing this chapter was the day of that lunch. The universe just winked at me ;)

I cannot wait for you to experience these God-winks! You will get goose bumps; the hair on the back of your neck will stand up. The joy of it will bring tears to your eyes. My heart swells with gratitude each time. Those synchronicities will get so frequent, and seem so absolutely unbelievable, that you will start to shake your head and smile.

As you awaken, prepare for amazing changes in your life. Some may seem difficult or sad in the moment. All of them will further you on your path of spiritual awakening.

Every single one of them is an experience that you are meant to have. You will become a better human being because of these experiences.

EPILOGUE

"Evil (ignorance) is like a shadow—it has no real substance of its own; it is simply a lack of light. You cannot cause a shadow to disappear by trying to fight it, stamp on it, by railing against it, or any other form of emotional or physical resistance. In order to cause a shadow to disappear, you must shine light on it." - Shakti Gawain

Living your best life is more than attainable. It is expected. You came here to this Earth to learn how to attain it. You are not meant to be unhappy. You are loved. You are love. Our true nature is that of pure love. We have to come to understand and remember that we are pure unconditional love. We just have to step into the light and follow the path of our spiritual awakening.

The ingredients in my spiritual recipe won't be appealing to everyone. As I leave you, please know that some of the practices I've described will work for some people and not for others. You can see what works for you and stick with those. But keep your heart and your mind open to the possibility that even though you don't think something is going to work for you at this moment, don't forget to come back to it later. You may be surprised.

Once those little seeds are planted into your subconscious, your conscious has no other choice but to bring them to fruition.

Bless you on your beautiful journey.

Namaste

If you would be so kind as to go to your favorite site, and leave a review of my book I would be truly grateful :)

www.spiritualrecipe.com

Made in the USA
Las Vegas, NV
12 October 2021